For **Sam** and **Mabel**
My Shining Stars

It was a splendid, sunny day.
Freddie the Frog, was leaping along
his merry little way.

As he scruffled atop his lily pad, he blinked his eyes to see....

Well he saw a butterfly fluttering.
Her mouth it was a muttering....

"Oh me, Oh my! Whatever shall I do?" cried Bibelle!
"My wings fell in. I cannot swim! Who will come to my rescue?"

Now Freddie the Frog, plopped down on the log,
where Bibelle was floating away.

He reached gently down.
Scooped her wings in his arms.
And rescued her all in a day!

"Oh me, Oh my! You are clever through and through" bragged Bibelle.

"I muttered and I sputtered.
Yes! I cried and sighed. That's true.
Still, you came to my rescue!"

Freddie the Frog kind of blushed with a nod,
And tumbled out words best he could.

"Well you would do the same for me,
as I just did for you."

Freddie the Frog said "Bibelle, here's a trick.
It will dry your wings in a jiff!"

"Just climb on my back.
Feel the Crickety Crack.
And soak up the sun's warm rays.
Before you know why, your wings will be dry.
And we'll sing Happy Hip Hip Hooray!" ~♫

Bibelle slowly fluttered.
Her wings rather sputtered,
then lifted her high in the sky!

She Swiveled and Swirled
And then Tumbled and Twirled
How Splendiferously Fun! Me oh My!

Now Freddie the Frog scampered log after log, frantically shouting "Bibelle, please come back!"

He never met a butterfly that could
dance in the sky. "Why oh why did she fly away?
I'll never see her again," Freddie cried.

Now Freddie the Frog plopped down on his pad.
He was so very sad, indeed.

He helped Bibelle mend
as she rounded the bend, but, alas,
now he's lost his best friend.

Just then in the thicket
He heard a lone cricket say
"Freddie, look up to the sky!"

And there came Bibelle
in all of her glory! Bursting and
Bouncing forth fanciful stories!

She swooped way down low and kissed Freddie "Hello."
He hopped up and down with great joy!

"I'm thrilled you are here.
I so missed you my dear.
Your wings sure do magical things!"

Now Freddie the Frog
and Bibelle the Butterfly
seem to travel a lot these days.

Yet where they love most,
is "Home Sweet Home", with Family,
Friends, and Fun days!.

You can see them together,
nestled close to each other, safe
and warmed by the sun's setting rays.

The End

A big, heartfelt "Thank You" to all our "Book Angels",
big and small, the "Lovely Hands", and "Smiling Faces".
You know who you are. XO

Copyright © 2015 by Carol Ann Ashley Birtwell

For more fun adventures with Freddie and Bibelle including free pages to color, audio recording of the book, Events for concerts and book signing and more, go to:

FreddieandBibelle.com
858 205 8374 mamalushka@gmail.com

Made in the USA
San Bernardino, CA
20 February 2015